M000164557

IRISH BLESSINGS, TOASTS & CURSES

PADRAIC O'FARRELL

MERCIER PRESS

MERCIER PRESS
Cork
www.mercierpress.ie

© Estate of Padraic O'Farrell, 2019

Taken from *Before the Devil Knows You're Dead,* first published in 1993. This edition published 2019.

ISBN: 978 1 78117 696 2

A CIP record for this title is available from the British Library

Printed and bound in the EU.

CONTENTS

BLESSINGS

It is difficult to realise that not so many years ago little of our everyday business was undertaken without the benefit of God's blessing invoked by ourselves or others. Going to fish or save turf, hearing news of a death or marriage, consoling neighbours in sorrow or sharing their joy – there was a particular blessing for every occasion and people uttered these ejaculations without fear of being considered passé or over-religious. Some of these habits have survived. The simple 'God bless you', 'God save you' or 'God rest his soul' are heard as often as they are mocked, at least.

Many of the following blessings are translated from the Irish; others are remembered from a rural childhood. All have their own charm.

Animals, Birds, etc.

The blessing of Mary, the blessing of God
The blessing of sun, moon and road;
Of man from the east, of man from the west,
My blessing on you – be you blest.

(*Said when milking.*)

May the holes in your nets be no larger than
the fish in it.

Here's to the grey goose
With the golden wing;
A free country
And a Fenian king.

(*IFC Ms, vol. 583, p. 276*)

May you be Christ's ghillie and the trout leppin'.

God bless three times with three spits for luck.
(*Said at the birth of livestock.*)

May there be a fox on your fishing-hook, and a hare on your bait.

Death

Ar dheas Dé go raibh a anam.
(*May his soul be on the right hand of God.*)

May I never kill a person and may nobody kill me. But if someone thinks of killing me, may I kill him.

(*From the Irish.*)

May God grant you a generous share of eternity.

God's blessing be on the souls of the dead and may we be a long time following them.

That you may never be left to die a sinner.

May the grass on the road to hell grow long.

Blessed Virgin, God's own mother,
Shining light set up on high,
Candle blazing in the heavens,
Be with me the day I die.
(*Douglas Hyde*)

Oh Brigid, Mary of the Gael,
Oh Brigid, extend your aid;
Keep me under your protection from all harm
Until I die in the companionship of God.

To Christ the seed
To Christ the harvest
In God's haggard
May we meet.
(*From the Irish.*)

May God level the road for his soul.

May you have a smith's *meitheal* at your wake.
(*Meitheal: a big crowd.*)

May you and yours be farthest from the grave.

On your deathbed, may you have the grace of God and of your neighbours.

May St Michael have a blast in his eye and the Devil without ballast on your Judgement Day.
(*St Michael was said to weigh good deeds, the devil bad ones.*)

May there be rain at your funeral.
(*Considered a good omen.*)

When you reach the inn of death, I hope it's closing time.

Health and Welfare

God's bounty to you and your stock.

May you never bear the heavy load of an empty stomach.

Saol fada agus breac–shláinte chugat.
(*Long life and middling health to you.*)

May white snuff be at your wake,
Bakers bread and curran-y cake
And plinty on your table, late and soon.
(*John B. Keane*, Sive, *Act 1, Scene 3*)

May you only grow old in the face
Be treasured and cared for with grace.

Mary and her son, Brigid and her cloak, God
and His strength between you and pestilence.
(*Or some named disease.*)

Bless you and your clan, and may every limb
of your body be as strong as the Fianna's stick.
(*From the Irish.*)

May you have rye bread to do you good,
Wheaten bread to sweeten your blood,
Barley bread to do you no harm
And oatmeal bread to strengthen your arm.

My thousand blessings and God's blessing on
you and may you never want for anything.

The face of life and health, and the beating of
all be yours.

Seven times the full of St Patrick's graveyard,
Seven times the full of the tomb of Christ,
Seven times the full of the well of grace,
Of blessings on you until we see each other
    again.

Bright glorious May
And my thousand blessings to you;
The best doctor's medicine to you
In sickness or in health.

May you escape the gallows, avoid distress,
and be as healthy as a trout.

My best, biggest and flouriest potatoes to you.

The five loaves and the two fishes of the five thousand be with God's people always.

That your stirabout may always go 'puff puff' and never 'clip clap'.
(*May it not be watery, i.e. may you have plenty.*)

May springtime never be far away for you.

May I see you grey and your clan sensible.

Peace on your hand and health to all who shake it.

Whatever takes longest to come to you, may it be worth waiting for.

May your barn be always full,
Free from fox and crow and gull.

May big headaches and little fevers stay far from you always.

The strength of St Patrick's horse to you.

May you live as long as you want and never want as long as you live.

God between us and all harm.
(*Also used in sympathy about another's misfortune.*)

That you may never comb a grey head.

May you have health to wear it.
(*Said on seeing a new garment being worn.*)

A blessing will not fill the stomach but take it anyhow.

God spare you the years to smoke your dudeen, drink your cruiskeen, flourish your alpeen to wallop a spalpeen.

Nár laga Dia thú.
(*May God not weaken you.*)

Never a *guí gann* in your life.
(*Scarce blessing. A prayer only for friends.*)

To the doctor may you never hand any money,
And sweet be your hand in a pot full of honey.

The health of the risen to you.

May there never be a rattle in your skillet.

May you never see the bottom of your pot.

That your griddle may always be hot.

May you never be beyond cutting a flitch.

That the face of all good news and the back of all bad news be towards you.

May you have a gentleman for a landlord.

That God may give you the back to bear the burden.

More power to your elbow.

May the strength of three be in your journey through life.

May you never see a poor day.

The Lord keep you in his hand but never close his fist too tight on you.

God's help be always nearer than the door for you.

Glory be to God on high
Only for the bit we ate we'd die!
Prayer and fasting are good for a sinner
But a hungry man would want his dinner.

Light in your eyes,
Teeth in your mouth,
Thatch on top.
Flesh on you,
Bone on you,
Legs and feet under you,
And a tail behind to guide you.

The look of Mary, the look of God take this
headache away.

Home

God bless the corners of this house
And be the lintel blessed.
Bless the hearth, the table too
And bless each place of rest.
Bless each door that opens wide
To stranger, kith and kin;
Bless each shining window-pane
That lets the sunshine in.
Bless the roof-tree up above
Bless every solid wall.
The peace of man, the peace of love,
The peace of God on all.

(*Featured on pictures that hung in kitchens many years ago.
Origin unknown.*)

Bless my humble kitchen, Lord,
I love its every nook.
Bless me as I toil in it
About my daily work.
Bless the meals that I prepare
Grant seas'ning from above.
Bestow Thy blessing and Thy grace
And most of all, your love.
As we prepare to eat our meal
May you the table spread,
Let us not forget to thank you, Lord
For all our daily bread.
So bless my humble kitchen, Lord,
And all who enter it;
Bless them with joy and peace and love
As happily they sit.

(*Ditto*)

May the blessing of the five loaves and two
fishes that God divided among five thousand
be ours, and may the King who divided place
pot luck in our food and in our portion.
(*Said before meals.*)

May your woman be a strong woman,
May your cows be white,
And may your house be on a height.

Said to have been uttered by St Patrick, who also used the
reverse as a curse:

May your woman be an ugly woman,
May your cows be black beasts
And may your house be in a valley.

(Béaloideas, *Iml. V, Uimh. 1, Meitheamh, 1935*)

Bless this house, O Lord we pray
Make it safe by night and day.
Bless these walls so firm and stout,
Keeping want and trouble out.
Bless the roof and chimneys tall
Let Thy peace lie over all
Bless the doors that they may prove
Ever open to joy and love.
Bless the windows, shining bright
Letting in God's heavenly light
Bless the hearth a blazing there
With smoke ascending like a prayer.
Bless the people here within,
Keep them pure and free from sin;
Bless us all that we may be
Fit O Lord, to dwell with Thee.
Bless us all that we, one day,
May dwell, O Lord with thee.

God guard this home from roof to floor
The Twelve Apostles guard the door;
Four good angels round each bed,
Two at the foot and two at the head.

Bless us, O Lord, and these thy gifts which of
Thy bounty we are about to receive, through
Christ Our Lord.

(*Grace before meals.*)

The sweet protection of the three sons – the
son of God, Mac Duagh and Mac Dara on
all here.

Love and Marriage

O woman loved by me, may you give me your
heart, your soul and your body.
(*Said close by a mill-wheel, stream and tree as the man
presents butter on a new plate to the girl.*)

May you never be a blue bride, allanah.
(*In the west of Ireland a 'Shrove Tuesday bride', i.e. one
who was pregnant and forced to marry, was called a blue
bride.*)

May your partner be his own man to the
power of two.

May you sleep in your man's dirty nightshirt and not rue it.

(*Such sleep was said to win the man's heart.*)

That your love knot may be sealed with heaven's wax.

Help and deliverance and friendship of God on you both. God grant you a gradle of joy.

(*Wedding blessing. Gradle means 'great deal'.*)

May your peltin' paper be a hundred pound note.

(*Peltin' paper: document of consent to marry from a priest.*)

You for me and I for thee and never another.
Your face turned to mine and away from all
others.

(*Said secretly by a woman after offering a drink to her
man.*)

May the health that got you for us leave you
healthy with us, with the help of God and the
light of his grace.

(*Said by a couple when their child is born.*)

The blessing of the saints and angels
The blessing of anyone else who knows us;
And my own blessing, without stain, to you
Until the Kingdom of Glory.

(*From the Irish. Said at betrothal.*)

By the power that Christ brought from heaven, may you love me, woman. As the sun follows its course, may you follow me. As light to the eye, as bread to the hungry, as joy to the heart, may your presence be with me, woman that I love, till death comes to part us asunder.

O Christ, by your five wounds, by the nine orders of angels, if this woman is ordained for me let me grasp her hand and breathe her breath. *Mo grádh*, I place a talisman to your crown, to the sole of your foot, to each of your breasts so that you may never leave or forsake me. As the foal after the mare, as the child after the mother, follow me and stay with me until death do us part.

May you marry an orphan.

(*i.e. may you never have trouble from in-laws.*)

May you never marry a whistling woman.

(*Regarded as evil.*)

Go maire sibh bhur saol nua.

(*Marriage congratulation: may you enjoy your new life.*)

That your wife may knit for infants and may her needles always click after dark.

(*Such knitting was thought to be best, because sheep were asleep then.*)

Come now listen while I sing
To the blessing that I bring
To the bridegroom and his lovely bride so fair.
May they dwell in wedded joy
May they ever hear the cry
Of a new big bouncing baby every year.
(*John B. Keane*, Sive, *Act 2, Scene 2*)

May your banns be read by a bishop.

May your bodies please each other like the stars do their Master.

A golden ring on your swollen body.
(*Said to a pregnant woman.*)

The blessing that Mary placed on the butter
The blessing for love and perpetual endearment:
That your body will not cease
Its awareness of mine;
That your love continues to follow my face
As the calf follows the cow
From this day to the day of my death.
(*From the Irish.*)

May the man that you marry never have an
old maid for a mother.

May your bed be soft and your man's hand
along with it.

Sweet be her hand on you as if it came out of a pot of honey.

May your man never rise from an unfinished Mass, from food without offering grace, or from yourself for another woman.

Sliocht sleachta ar shliocht bhur sleachta.
(*May there be a generation of children on your children's children.*)

May you never be sent to the gander paddock.
(*Be in your wife's bad graces.*)

Love, life and happiness; may your troubles be few and your blessings plenty.

Be there always a man's shirt on your clothes-line.

Ye pow'rs who over love preside,
Since mortal beauties drop so soon,
If you would have us well supplied,
Send us new nymphs with each new moon.
(*Jonathan Swift, 'The Progress of Beauty'*)

May your woman never burn her coal without heating herself.

Miscellaneous

May you never cross a stream in brown flood, a patch of soft grass or an angry woman.

May we see the bright light of tomorrow.

May God give us food when we're hungry, money when we need it and heaven when we die.

If God sends you on a stony path, may he give you strong brogues (shoes).

God loves his own people; may they include you.

May your voice be above every other voice, that God may not strike down your care or your company.

May peace and plenty be first to lift the latch of your door and happiness be guided to your home by the Christmas candle.

May your hand be stretched out in friendship but never in want during the coming year.
(*A New Year blessing.*)

Go mbeirimid beo ar an am seo arís.
(*May we all be alive this time next year. Said at the Christmas meal and other annual celebrations.*)

The blessing of God's only Son who has purchased us dearly be on your trade.

God prevent the evil eye from ever falling on you.

Sand from heaven's shore in the eye of your enemy.

May your enemies never hear you.

Good health to the bearer of good news and may bad news be far from you.

May you never see or hear what you hear or see, or cut your throat with your tongue.

Go n-eírí an bóthar leat.
(*Safe journey. Lit: May the road rise with you.*)

Go n-eírí an t-ádh leat.
(*Good luck attend to you.*)

The light of heaven to all things gone and may they never come back to haunt us.

May God increase your neighbours – those of them that are useful to you.

(*From the Irish.*)

God save all here bar the cat.

(*Said upon entering a house. It was considered unlucky to bless the cat.*)

God settle you and your trouble.

May the wind be always at your back.

May you have a full moon on a dark night and the road downhill to your door.

Help and grace and friendship from God be on all here.

Ten thousand blessings upon all that's here ...
(*John M. Synge*, The Playboy of the Western World, *Act III*)

Céad míle fáilte romath.
(*A hundred thousand welcomes to you.*)

The light of heaven shine on you.

Take the world free and easy and may it take you the same.

If you have tears, may they turn God's mill-wheel.

May you have warm words on a cold evening.

May you be poor in misfortune, rich in blessings, slow to make enemies, fast to make friends; but rich or poor, slow or fast, may you know only happiness from this day out.

May God speak sweetly of you.

May God tarry with you.
or God go with you always.

May God take you past the evil hour without loss or pain.

May you live till we see you again.

The hand of God rest lightly on you.

Nollaig faoi shéan is faoi shonas duit.
(*A prosperous and happy Christmas to you.*)

God bless the work.
Answer: And you too.

Self-Blessings

O countenance brighter than the sun, do not allow me to be long in pain.
(*Douglas Hyde*)

Health of the night's sleep to us.
(*Ibid.*)

I lie with God; may He lie with me.

May sin and loss be kept from me during the course of this day.

May I be kissed by all in red petticoats and
check aprons between Kenmare and Killarney.

May I always meet my fetch at morning.
(*Considered lucky.*)

Kindle inside my heart, O Lord
The spark of love
For my enemies, relatives and friends.
(*From the Irish.*)

May Jesus be at my head,
The Virgin at my feet
The Twelve Apostles round my bed
When I am fast asleep.

Jesus this hour I give to Thee
For all the past hour pardon me.
know that I shall soon depart
So hide me in Thy Sacred Heart.
(*Said on the hour, every hour.*)

If I'm a bigger liar than the clock in Strabane itself, let me be truthful to my friends.

Bless me, Lord, defend and govern me and after this short and miserable pilgrimage bring me to everlasting life.

May the name of Jesus be firmly inscribed in the middle of my heart.

Long eaters are long livers, so let not my
dinner be over before I get it.

May I always do God's business.

Son of the world, may your Father bless and
save me always.

Mary of Grace
Mother of the Son of God
May you take me in your care this day.

O Brigid, Mary of the Gael, wrap me in your
cloak.

I rise with Christ
May Christ rise with me;
The hand of God around me
Asleep or awake.

May God's bounty and St Patrick's blessing
be with me.

God give me health, wealth and happiness but
make sure they don't make me sick, poor and
miserable.

That I may have the richness of health and
know it.

If my neighbour has knowledge, let me not be
too proud to light my candle from it.

May I be taught from the book of God.

I call on the seven daughters of the ocean
Who knit the stitches of the sons of longevity.
May three deaths be taken from me,
Three lifetimes given to me,
Seven waves of good fortune bestowed on me!
May spectres not harm me during my journey
Without hindrance, in Laserian's breastplate
May my name not be promised in vain!
May old age be mine
And death not come to me until I reach it.

(*From the Irish.*)

May we always have the love of God and of the neighbours.

May God leave us healthy until a year from today.

May God and His Holy Mother save us at the hour of death.

God between us and all harm.
or God between us and the evil spirit.

May God save us from the evil intentions of others.

Eternal Father, let your protective shield guard us night and day.

Faoi bhrat Bhríde sinn!
(*May we be under Brigid's cloak.*)

May God not quench the light of heaven on us.

Get for me, O Mother Mary,
A son before I go from this world.
Do not delay to put his seed in my blood,
O Womb in which the humanity of God was
    formed.
(*Giolla Brighde Ó hEoghusa, 'A Prayer'*)

May I live till I'm old and serve the God who rules heaven and may a welcome await me in eternal Paradise.

(*Translated and adapted from James Carney.*)

May I never take life too seriously, knowing I'll never get out of it alive.

People, Places and Politics

Blessings of Granny Doherty,
She was the stuff;
She hunted the Orangemen
Over the bluff.

Angels of heaven bless the bare flags of Aran.

Athenry that was, Galway that is and Aran that will be, God bless us all.

May the Lord in His mercy be kind to Belfast.
(*Maurice Craig, 'Ballad to a Traditional Refrain'*)

May the shadow of John Redmond never fall on your sons.
(*i.e. may they never be recruited for the British Army.*)

Bless the men from Ballinglen, put whiskey in my tay (tea).

May every Mayoman's pile be as high as
Croagh Patrick and may his sorrows be as
scarce as elephants in Murrisk.

Bless the men from Kerry,
And bless the men from Clare,
Those on the Aran islands,
The fine men from Kildare.
Bless the lads from Wicklow,
From Donegal as well;
From the whole damned part of Ireland
And the rest can go to hell.

God bless the grey mountains of dark Donegal
God bless royal Aileach, the pride of them all.
(*Charles Gavan Duffy, 'Inishowen'*)

Here's a health to you, Father O'Flynn
Sláinte and *sláinte* and *sláinte* again.
(*A. P. Graves*)

Ireland, long a province, be a nation once again.
(*Thomas Davis*)

May the stones of Tory never point at you.
(*It was believed that the 'Cursing Stones' of Tory brought bad luck if pointed at an enemy.*)

May you have a Keogh for a neighbour.
(*Blood from a Keogh was alleged to have healing properties.*)

Up the rebels, to Hell with the Pope,
And God Save – as you prefer – the King or
  Ireland.

(*Louis MacNeice, 'Autumn Journal XVI'*)

Various Occasions

Most of the following are loosely translated from
Béaloideas, *Iml. XIV, pp. 130–155 where they ap-*
peared in Irish. Some were used only in the Teelin,
Co. Donegal, area, but others were used widely.

May God save yourself and your crew from
drowning.

(*Said to fishermen going to sea.*)

The peace of God with my soul!
(*Said in astonishment on hearing of some marvel.*)

Good luck be on your hand and may you not die in sin and may you never sprain your hand that shared with the poor.
(*Said by a person who receives alms.*)

May God give you luck and may the fish of the great sea face you.
(*Said to fishermen.*)

May God save you from harm.
(*Said when a favour is done.*)

May God bring you safely home and give you
every sort of luck.

(*Uttered to fishermen going to sea.*)

May God and His Holy Mother save us from
the power of fire and water.

(*Uttered on hearing thunder.*)

Rath Dé ort!

(*Meaning 'the grace of God on you'. Said in thanks.*)

A thousand blessings with the name of Paul.

(*Said when speaking about a person with epilepsy, which
was called Paul's disease.*)

God grant that you do what is best.
(*Said to a person who has a serious decision to make.*)

Do not come between the hope of God.
(*Said when bad weather threatens the saving of crops or turf, or the catching of fish.*)

May God leave them to you.
(*Said on meeting a parent accompanied by children.*)

God's blessing on you.
(*Said to a person with a sore on a limb.*)

May God deliver him (from an illness).

May God never limit you.
(*Uttered as encouragement to someone who has failed in any way.*)

May God place a hand on him.
(*Said about a person who is so sick that he would be better off dead.*)

The Cross of the Crucifixion of Christ be on you.
(*Uttered by a mother while making the sign of the Cross on a child not yet able to do so himself.*)

May God settle him.
(*Said of a person in trouble.*)

God give you the price.
(*Said to a person who has accomplished something worth-while.*)

May God increase your store and save those who are minding you.
(*Said to somebody who has received an unexpected wind-fall.*)

May God and Mary save us and all belonging to us from the evil of the night.
(*Said at the end of the recitation of the Rosary.*)

May your abode please you.
(*Said to somebody who moves house.*)

God's gift to you.
(*Said to a musician or other talented person who has entertained.*)

May you receive the weight of your alms of God's grace.
(*Said in thanks by a person who receives alms.*)

May God put fruit and blossom on the seed we are about to sow.
(*Uttered as potato sets are taken down for sowing.*)

May God leave health to all we see.
or May God leave health to your stock.
(*Uttered when meeting someone driving stock.*)

May your journey rise with you and may God give you luck.

(*Said to somebody about to emigrate.*)

Bloom and blessing, night and day, on you.

(*Said, especially to children, when a good turn is done.*)

May God save you without the devil.
or May God make it easy on you.

(*Said to people in trouble.*)

May your soul find eternal glory.

(*Said in thanks for help.*)

The shape of Christ be on his coat.

(*Uttered when somebody good or holy is mentioned or seen.*)

May all your bad luck go with him.

(*Said to a neighbour on burying a beast of his.*)

May God give us enough body and soul to bear our cross patiently.

(*Said when a bereavement or other catastrophe occurs in a family.*)

The fruit of your hand, O God, on this year's crops.

(*Said when digging the first of the new potatoes.*)

God and Mary bless you, motherless child,
Your cry is not so sweet, nor is your laughter
   bright.
(*Aindrias Ó Muimhneacháin*)

The King of the World, King of Brightness,
King of Heaven and Paradise, King of Saints
born in the stable bless all here.
(*Said on entering a house on Christmas Eve.*)
Answer: May the same King bless you.

May your man not forsake the home on
Christmas night.
(*It was considered unlucky to do so.*)

May not more numerous be
The grains of sand by the sea,
Or the blades of grass on the lea,
Or the drops of dew on the tree,
Than the blessings upon the soul
And the souls of the dead with thee,
And my soul when life shall flee.

(*Said after smoking. Douglas Hyde*)

Amusing Blessings

Bless de Valera and Seán MacEntee,
Bless their brown bread and their half ounce
    of tea.

(*From a wartime parody commenting on food rationing.*)

Many happy returns of the day and may it miss you when it comes.

That you may never see a bad day and if it sees you may it be wearing glasses.

Good luck to you, your blood is worth bottling and may glass splinters blind hell's stokers.

May the wind be always at your back, especially coming home on Saturday night.

Ireland is rearing them yet and when she's done may you wed the best of them.

A thousand blessings, maybe more,
Come down on you, *mo grádh, mo stór;*
Especially if you give your hand
To tend me and my plot of land.

May you live to be a hundred years and one
extra year to atone.

Bless the man who ploughs the furrow;
Ferrets rabbits from a burrow.
Bless his wife, may she not often
Ferret his last penny off him.

May you always keep out from the priests;
that way you will keep in with them.

If you marry, may you marry last year.

Saints of glory protect us,
Holy Angels from the throne of God, guide
    us,
And if the devil still gets within a stone's
    throw of us
May there be nothing but sand to peg (throw)
    at us.

May St Peter never ask you to light a fire on a
lake or advise a headstrong woman.

May you be as well as you can bear to be.

May the hand that offers trouble be as idle as the left hand of a *bodhrán*.

May the lips that speak ill of you never say thanks to St Peter.

Bless the horse that farts at noon,
Twice bless the one that farts at eve,
And thrice bless the work that makes him fart.

May you find a good *sonuachar* (spouse) – what my mother-in-law's son got.
(*A woman who says this praises herself.*)

Let your enemies hear the bees but may you get the honey.

That your patch of trouble may not cover the hole in a leprechaun's breeches.

May you get what you're after with the help of God and two policemen.

May your horse always stand in the middle of the fair.

TOASTS
AND HEARTY WISHES

Whiskey, you're the divil,
You're leading me astray;
Over hills and mountains,
And to Americay.
You're sweeter, stronger, dacenter;
You're spunkier nor tay.
Oh whiskey, you're me darlin' drunk or sober!

Wet your whistle well and may we never die
of the drought!

In a chapter called 'Sláinte' from his book Irish Life and Lore, *Séamas Ó Catháin imparts valuable information on Irish toasts. These are not of the stuffy nature observed at formal dinners, but are genuine expressions of good fellowship and heartiness:*

'Here's health.' (*Seo do shláinte*)
Answer: 'God grant you health.' (*Sláinte ó Dhia duit*)

Good health boys, one and all, and may God bless you and the work. (*Bhur sláinte uilig go léir, a bhuachaillí, agus go gcuirí Dia rath oraibh féin agus ar bhur gcuid oibre.*)

Eternal rest to the soul that has joined the host of the dead.

(*At funerals.*)

Here's your health, may God give you luck and a safe journey and may God save the man that's going to settle down, from heartbreak, harm and need.

The next six toasts are from the Irish Folklore Collection as quoted in Ó Catháin's book:

Here's to you as good as you are,
And to me as bad as I am;
I'm as good as you are,
Bad and all as I am.

Here's to the pigeon of the green wing,
A Roman priest and a Fenian king,
Here's to King William
With a knife in his heart and a fork in his
    liver,
That he may never die or no one kill him,
Till he goes to hell and the devil gets 'melling'
    him.

Here's from the roof rib to the foundation
    stone,
All sorts of bother and misfortune,
Hell's blazes and damnation to any man who
    has a daughter –
And won't give her to me.

The health of bright glory to you.

Here's health and prosperity,
To you and all your posterity,
And them that doesn't drink with sincerity
That they may be damned for all eternity.

Here's to the High Son who stretched his
limbs for crucifixion on the cross, and here's
the health of the Virgin Mother, and here's
the health of St Patrick who blessed Ireland.

Sláinte!
(*[Your] health!*)

Praise God, all true Protestants
And I will toast no further
For had the Papists won the day,
There'd have been bloody murder.
(*Toast based on the nineteenth-century ballad 'The Boyne
Water'.*)

Good health to your enemies' enemies.

Hold your hour and have another!

Mo grá thú!
(*My love to you!*)

The health of the salmon and the trout
That swim to and fro' near the Bull's Mouth;*
Do not ask for a pot, mug or jug,
Down the hatch – drink up!
(*In Achill.)

Have another drink and may St Peter think
it's tay!

Drink, as in bumpers past troubles we drown,
A health to the lads that made croppies lie
down.
(Anon., 'Croppies lie Down', an Orange ballad.)

Here's your health for consideration!

Health to you and yours; to mine and ours.

If mine and ours ever come across you and
   yours,

I hope that you and yours will do as much for
   mine and ours

As mine and ours have done for you and yours.

(*Not recommended for late-night toasts!*)

Here's to the next one and may you be granted
a trooper's pardon!

Drink up! It's always the next one that sickens
you.

Good luck whatever!

Whiskey is the life of man,
Whiskey Johnny!
Whiskey in an old tin can,
Whiskey for my Johnny.
(*Belfast docks toast.*)

Health and long life to you
Land without rent to you
A child every year to you
And may you die in Ireland.

Good health without a cold in your pipes!

Your good health from person to person and
if any person doesn't wish it, let him speak up!

Here's to the first drop – the one that destroys you; there's no harm at all in the last!

May they be drinking bog-water, while you're supping the *uisce beatha* (whiskey).

Here's one for the road and may you know every turning!

I'll drink and I'll drink and I'll drink to your
    health, love
And were you on board ship, I'd drink to you
    the better!

(*Sailors' toast, from the Irish.*)

Here's mud in one eye and a glint in the other!

Here's to the maiden of blushing fifteen;
Now to the widow of fifty!
Here's to the flaunting, extravagant quean,
And then to the housewife that's thrifty.
Let the toast pass, drink to the lass,
I'll warrant they'll find an excuse for the glass.
(*Richard Brinsley Sheridan,* The School for Scandal, *Act 3, Scene 2*)

Here's to the hand that made the ball,
That shot Lord Leitrim in Donegal.
(*A Donegal toast.*)

May we forget the bitterness of paying for it!

May the roof above us never fall in
And may us good companions beneath it
Never fall out.

Thirst begets thirst
So be getting yours first;
Good luck! Stay sane!
Down the dusty lane!

May the next drop make the grass grow long
on the road to hell for you!

The memory of the chestnut horse that broke
the neck of King William!

We'll toast Old Ireland!
Dear Old Ireland!
Ireland boys, Hurrah!
(*T. D. Sullivan, 'Song from the Backwoods'*)

Here's to the same again or something similar!

Sláinte an bhradáin agat – croí folláin agus gob
fliuch.
(*The health of the salmon to you – a sound heart and a wet*
mouth.)

Good luck to you and bad shoes to your advisers.

(*Said to a drinking companion who complains about drink being bad for a man.*)

Here's health and the drunk's curse on Killarney to the begrudgers!

Sláinte! And when the world's troubles are displayed on the floor, may you select your own.

Health! May your well never run dry!

When, from heaven God looks down
On your very last half-crown,
By a miracle, may it suddenly clink
'Gainst another one and ten,
Against twenty, twice again –
Just as long as you keep paying for the drink!

Your property stay with you; may you rear
children on it and may they be around to look
after you. Drink up now to ensure as much!

Peace on your hand!

May God never knock you down as long as
you keep putting them up!

Saint Patrick was a gentleman;
Through strategy and strength
He drove the snakes from Erin
A toast, then, to his health.
But not too many toasts, now
Or you'll lose your sense and then
Forget about Saint Patrick
And meet all those snakes again.

Proposal: To healthy stock and may they never
need saving!
Reply: During drinking hours!

I'll give you your health and may your enemies
be beggars!

The face of the sad story be turned away from us!

Proposal: May you flourish like the fern!
Reply: God let you profit!

Your life and your health to you!

When you drop down from it (the drink) may there be the seventh son of a seventh son beside you ere the glass hits the floor.

May there never be a welt on the hand that pays for the drinks.

The health of all salmon,
The health of all trout
That swim back and forth
Near the wide river mouth.
Ask not for a saucepan,
A jug or a cup;
Down the hatch, my fine hero
Drink! Drink it all up!

Health to the man who buys his round
To heaven's alehouse be he bound.

Here's your health from the heel to the back
of the knee, and may we not leave this place
until we are drunk.
(*From the Irish.* Béaloideas, *Iml. XIV, p. 142*)

If you're on your ear before you leave, may it be hearing sweet words of comfort.

May you live as long as you want
And never want as long as you live.

May we always have a clean shirt, a clear conscience and a few bob in our pockets.
Answer: Or if not, a decent man to stand us a drink!

Drink as if it was your last one, but may the last one not come till morning.

May you be poor in misfortune,
Slow to make enemies
Fast to make friends
But rich or poor, slow or fast
May you know nothing but happiness.

At the end of the day,
Let us drink to work well done
And if you are an idler,
We'll toast tomorrow's fun.

A true man like you, man
Will lift your glass with us!
(*John Kells Ingram, 'The Memory of the Dead'*)

May we die happy by living to see our own funerals.

Here's a health to youze who waves the Union
    Jack
If youze pays for us who wears the Green;
Buy another round and here's your health
    again
And we'll all sing *God Save the Queen!*

O long life to the man who invented poteen
Sure the Pope ought to make him a martyr;
If I myself was this moment Victoria, our
    Queen,
I'd drink nothing but whiskey and water.

(*Michael Moran [Zozimus], 'In Praise of Poteen'*)

May God hold you in the hollow of His hand
and have a drink in the other for you.

We have our health, we have our memories,
we have our wives to bring us home.

(*Seán Nicholson, August 1992*)

Good luck to us all and bad luck to nobody.

CURSES

Animals, Birds, etc.

A fox on your fishing hook.
(Claddagh fisherman's curse. Patrick C. Power)

The plight of the boiled and broken minnow
to you.

May you buy every hair in your cow's tail.
(Pay dearly for stock.)

May your hens get the disorder, your cows the crippen (phosphorosis) and your calves the white scour and may you yourself go blind so that you'll not know your woman from a haystack.

(*Edited from IFC Ms, vol. 1403*)

May you find the bees but miss the honey.

Curse of the crows on you.

May the man who would curse the bladder out of a goat have a chat with you before Christmas.

May you hang a dog and drown a bitch.

A magpie on your wheatfield gate.

Black cows to you.

May all the goats in Gorey chase you to hell.

May the back of you get a salmon's roasting.

May your horse have a sagging nosebag.

May the ass that pulls your coffin-cart have no cross on its back.

If ever you're on the pig's back, I hope it's heading for the curing-house.

Garlacon (a lingering disease) to your stock.

That your cat may bury you with its clap.

The curse of the goose that lost the quill that wrote the ten commandments on you.

Death

That you may die roarin' like Doran's ass.

That your bread may be baked.
(*That you may die.*)

For many a day may you rest in the clay.

Six horse-loads of burial clay on you.

May there be red ribbons at your funeral.
(*Red ribbons were once worn at obsequies of a murder victim.*)

May they sing *Eileen Aroon* at your wake.

(*Considered an unlucky song.*)

May there never be enough of your people in heaven to make a half-set.

May the company at your wake pray on cold flags.

(*You will not get many prayers said for you.*)

Hungry grass grow around your grave.

(*Nobody had walked on it, therefore no prayers would be said.*)

May you never be buried in the pound section.

You mean thing! May you soon find out there's no pockets in a shroud.

May you not see the corncrake or the cuckoo.

Cripples and crooks carry your coffin.

That you may be a load for four before the year is out.

(*Four coffin-bearers.*)

That you may fester in your grave.

May the foam of the river settle on you.
(*May you drown.*)

May you die without a priest in a town with no clergy.

May there be a corpse here each Monday morning.
(*Said to have been uttered to St Patrick by a Corkman. The saint replied: 'May it be a starling's.'*)

May you rot in the pauper's plot.

May the only tears at your graveside be the onion-pullers'.

A slippy handle on your *sleán*.
(*If a* sleán *fell, it was believed that a family death would follow.*)

May the snails devour his corpse,
And the rain do harm worse;
May the devil sweep the hairy crature soon;
He's as greedy as a sow;
As the crow behind the plough;
That black man from the mountain, Seánín
    Rua!
(*John B. Keane*, Sive, *Act 1, Scene 3*)

Health and Wealth

May you have a little skillet,
May you have little in it.
May you have to break it,
To find the little bit in it.

May your spuds be like rosary-beads on the
stalk.

If your crop is tall
Be your *meitheal* small.
May the only gold you ever win
Be that what sticks to the callow's whin.

At the going down of the sun may you have nothing in your bag and less in your pocket.

That your pocket may drag your face into tripping you up.
(*i.e. that your wealth may bring you unhappiness.*)

May you some day follow the crow for your supper and get bitten by a jackdaw.

The hand of God fall on you and your money.

May you never see the light of heaven till you pay me what you owe me.

Stillborn or dawny (miserable, weak) stock to you.

May you live to see the two days.
(*Said to a wealthy person, wishing poverty.*)

Hell and the Devil

May the devil behead all landlords and make a day's work of their necks.

May you dance with a devil on your back.

The devil take you.

That the midil may tasp you, you glodach crois
ould beoir.
(*Tinkers' cant: That the devil may take you, you dirty old
woman.*)

May the seven terriers of hell sit on the spool
of your breast and bark in at your soul-case.
(*IFC Ms, vol. 1403*)

May the devil throw you into the pit of ashes
seven miles below hell.
(*John M. Feehan*)

May they all go to hell and not have a drop of porter to quench their eternal thirst.

May the devil weave your shroud and may he pin the seams together.
(*A double curse, since using pins in a shroud was considered unlucky.*)

That you may never see the inside of heaven.

The devil swallow you sideways.

To Halifax with you.
(*Here the word 'hell' is disguised.*)

Your soul to the devil.

Come hell or high water, may you be ruined.

The Old Boy settle your hash for you and have your guts for garters.

The devil fool you.

The devil tear you.

When the bottom falls out of Purgatory, may you join the poor Papists in hell.

May your next settle (bed) be at the hob of hell.

Hell's hottest corner for you.

The devil set a place for you in a hot contrary corner.

The devil's plague on you.

May the devil's coach-horse come at a canter to your wake.

Paddy Ryan's supper to you – hard knocks and
the devil to eat.

Well I hope that Old Nick,
Pokes your eyes with his stick.
Cuts your nose with a shears
And burns off your big ears.

May the devil damn you to the stone of dirges,
or to the well of ashes seven miles below hell;
and may the devil break your bones! And all
my calamity and harm and misfortune for a
year on you.

(*Patrick C. Power*)

The devil shake you by the heels.

That you may roast in hell for that and have your gravy sucked by the devil.

The devil's flame on you.

The devil's cagger (pedlar's haberdashery) on you.

May the keystone of heaven's arch fall on you and push you down below.

I'll carry you to the devil and may he take you out of my sight.

The tide of the devil engulf you.

May the devil break the hasp of your back.

(*James Joyce*)

Home

May you never call a hearth your own.

May you long be homeless.

May you never have more than point with your praties.

(*'Point' was just as much butter as would sit on the point of a knife.*)

Ill-Luck

Ill-luck to your mother for bearing you.

May your firstborn belong to the *lios* (*na sídhe*).

(*To the fairies.*)

A heart-scald on you.

May you go stone blind so that you won't know your wife from a headstone.
(*John M. Feehan*)

Harm and loss to you with lasting grief.

Scréach mhaidne chugat.
(*The morning screech on you.*)

May there be guinea-fowl crying at your child's birth.
(*A bad luck sign.*)

Monday's curse on you.

A high noose and gallows and a windy day outside (to you).

May you break your kneecap going down the steep steps of your rosiest garden.

May the bard's curse on the man who stole his harp fall on you.

Cold days and nights without a fire to you.

That you may meet your fetch at evening.
(*Believed to bring bad luck.*)

Bad cess to you.

May you wind up like Weakie Willy Walsh –
the breath only just in and out of him and the
grass not knowing he was walking over it.

May he screech with awful thirst
May his brains and eyeballs burst
That melted *amadán*, that big bostoon,
May the fleas consume his bed
And the mange eat up his head,
That blackman from the mountain, Seánín
    Rua.

(*John B. Keane, Sive, Act 2, Scene 2*)

Marriage

May you marry in haste and repent at leisure.

May you marry far from the ashpit.
(*A stranger.*)

Your eyes damp with tears
Your fingers trembling
Your body barren
Your breasts milkless
With never a son
Nor ever the strength
To please your man.

May you marry a wench that blows wind like
a stone from a sling.

May the Black Hag of Beara curse this
alliance.

May you marry a mountainy woman so that
you'll marry the whole mountain.

May she marry a ghost and bear him a kitten
    and may
The High King of glory permit her to get the
    mange.

(*James Stephens, 'A Glass of Beer'*)

May you marry a frigid widow-woman left a *bánóg* of thistles.

Pissmires and spiders be in your marriage-bed.

May you marry a Roman (and have to quit your place and disgrace your family).
(*An Orange curse.*)

May you have the runs on your wedding-night.

Morning screams to you.

In your house, may the grey mare be the better horse.
or May the long-haired chum lead your gallop.
(*May the woman be boss in your home.*)

Miscellaneous

A high windy gallows to you.
By the sod you stand on, curse not
You tread it but for a short while
But lie beneath it for eternity.
(*From the Irish. Retort to a curse uttered.*)

Curse of Cromwell on you.

The madness of the brain on him,
A broken heart in him,
A heart-scourge beside him,
A hangman's noose around him.

O wretch of the crooked foot, the crippled knee and the squinting eye, a thousand curses on you, torn clothes on your back and a pox on every bit of you.

Curse of God on you.

O cursed hag who prays not to Mary, may your teeth fall out and may you disappear across the sea.

Curse of Moll Anthony on you.

(*County Kildare curse.*)

Curse of Biddy Early on you.

(*County Clare curse.*)

Curse of Madge Moran on you.

(*County Meath curse.*)

May I bend a coin on the Holy Ghost for you.

(*Said as a sixpenny piece is hidden in a church to curse someone.*)

God's curse and His Church's be on you.

Curse of the seven snotty orphans on you.

A red nail through the tongue that said it.

Curse of the Seven Septs of the Laois Crosbies on you.

The seven curses of Quilty on you.

The curse of the O'Flahertys on you.
(*The line of the powerful Galway clan was discontinued because of a priest's curse.*)

Curse of the town on you.
(*Uttered by a tinker who spent all his money carousing in a particular town.*)

Curse of the wretched and the strong on the one who gave.

Devil damn you.

May the curse of the woman on the one who seduced her man fall on you.

Bad luck to them that's cloddin' stones.
(*Throwing stories – Belfast.*)

May God never give you his benefit.

Mallacht na Bantraí ort.
(*The widow's curse on you.*)

Son of God make you blind.

Your mouth and your face under you.
(*Be 'down in the mouth', therefore unhappy.*)

He can quench the candle at the other side of the kitchen with a curse and I hope he comes to your *céilí*.

Back of my hand to you.

The priest's curse on you.

Abiding hatred fall on you.

The curse of the White Woman on you.

Here's the dirty water to you.
or Poisoned destruction to you.
(*A curse on the fairies, when throwing out water.*)

May the gates of paradise never open to you.

The wretched state of the sinner and the gallows knot to you.

God take the east and west from you –
The road before and behind you.

Money and Poverty

The devil take your last shilling.

May your Sunday best have its share of turtles.
(*Threads hanging down – Antrim.*)

May your thatch leak,
And your boots squeak.
May your eyes forever squint
And may you never have the rint (rent).

That you may have forty-five ways of putting
on your coat this harvest-time.

(*i.e. be in tatters.*)

May all belonging to you have to live on the
smell of an oily rag.

That you may scratch a beggarman's back
some day.

(*i.e. be a beggar yourself.*)

Faith, may you follow the crow for that some day.

(*Uttered when seeing some food thrown away.*)

Faith, may you get your comeuppance before your pride wears down.

May you not have enough to buy your shroud.

People, Places and Politics

May the back of your shirt never pass Churchtown.

(*Said by a priest to a parishioner who vowed to vote Tory.*)

God damn the Whigs and Tories too.

(*Jonathan Swift, 'Mad Mullinix and Timothy'*)

If you take the king's shilling, may you spend it in hell.

Bad cess to that robber, old Cromwell, and to all his long battering train.

(*Anon., 'Blarney Castle, My Darling'*)

'Tis with the devil you will fly away, you porter-swiping similitude of the bisection of a vortex!

(*Anon., The Liberator and Biddy Moriarty*)

The dog's bark on the O'Keefes to you.

(*The O'Keefes were harsh landlords.*)

May the curse of the *maighdean mhara* (mermaid) on the O'Briens of Newhall plague you.

(*In the guise of a wonderful cow, the mermaid provided the people of Clare, except the O'Briens, with milk during the Famine.*)

The curse of the Mad Major on you.

(*Major Denis O'Farrell, whose cursing of an adjutant led Sir Charles Maxwell to state: 'I never heard a man cursed to my perfect satisfaction until I heard [the adjutant] anathematised in the Phoenix Park.' P. W. Joyce.*)

Jesus, sweet God and Father of the Lamb
Who sees us in shackles, too harshly bound,
Since you made us Christians from Friday till
    Monday morning
Shelter us and dismiss this scum from us.

(From the Irish. Spoken against British soldiers.)

Like the Clonmacnoise mason, may you never
finish what you set out to do.

(A reference to Clonmacnoise's unfinished round tower.)

The town of Naas is an awful place,
Kilcock is just as bad;
But of all the places I've ever been
Well curse [or worse expletive] you Kinnegad.

Damn the cardboard shields the Dominicans
used in Spain, those bloodstained bowsies.
(*Flann O'Brien*)

Curses, like chickens, come home to roost
And if you say 'Up Dev!' may you be clockin'!

Vote for pauper, vote for toff;
If you vote for the Blueshirts, may your hand
fall off.

Major Sirr, despised cur,
The Chief of Dublin's Peelers,
May Satan be your guest for tea
And all his evil dealers.

My curse on Straid; may there never be more
than one couple from one townland married
there.

(*Said to have been uttered by Colmcille.*)

My curse on you and Crossconnel and may it
never be without a fool.

(*Ditto*)

Bad luck to the people of Kerry
Bad luck to the men of Kildare
But the luck of the devil from hell
On the landlord O'Brien from Clare.

The curse of the twelve Biddies on you.

I call on you, oh stone,
To keep Breed below.
She kept us short of drink
And on our house brought shame.
And since, oh Breed, you're buried now,
Eternal thirst to you and drought.

(*Uttered by the poet Raftery at the grave of a mean housekeeper. Translated by Patrick C. Power.*)

My curse attend Dungarvan,
Her boats, her borough and her fish!
May every woe that mars man,
Come dancing down upon her dish!

(*Part of a curse uttered by a blind beggar robbed in Dungarvan. Padraic Colum.*)

Various Occasions

That your arm may get twisted as a bog blackthorn.

(*Uttered by wrestlers at hurling matches long ago.*)

Be the Dhalum seek sudil but I'll corib your jeel.

(*Tinker's cant: By the good God Almighty, I will kill you tonight.*)

Bad scran to those who pay the priest more heed than their neighbours.

(*Example of imprecation when religion was placed before vital help.*)

If she turns first may she take the road to hell.
(*Said at coursing matches.*)

May the sun get shy before he finishes.
(*Said when an enemy is about to go haymaking.*)

Tasp gut may luber you.
(*Tinkers' cant: The curse of God on you.*)

The Lord look down on the crackawly who did it.
(*Uttered after some destruction is done by a stupid person in Cork.*)

May hell's heat dry his lips, the mean mank.
(*Said when a dirty fellow [mank] dodges buying his round of drinks.*)

Blast the divil that brought you this way.
(*Said to an unwelcome stranger.*)

That it may choke you a mile from a well.
(*Said to someone who is eating or drinking but who does not offer hospitality.*)

That he may carry his traps in his trews.
(*Cork slang. May he carry all his belongings in his trouser pockets. Said in ill-will, especially if buying a drink is shirked.*)

Amusing Imprecations

May the devil catch you and take you to where you cannot be found.

May he be shot by a bullet or smothered in bed hungry.

May your heifer never get to the bull.

May the man who steals my flute lose the power of his limbs and never blow even soup.

Your skeleton and its two sons rout you.

May you be gummy by the time you have mate on your table.

May the devil's dowser dip his twig to your buttermilk.

The pus of a poxy fox in your whiskey.

Forty weasels chew your lights,
Perforate your bowels with bite
Till you're leaking like a colander of gruel.
May a ferret with a grin,
Lash its molars to your chin
As you scream in pain like Festy Flynn, the
    fool.

May you be torn in strips and have a rag for
a bonnet.

May muck-maggots gulp your guts,
Chew your fingers to the butts
Crawling in and out your navel, night and day;
And a hundred swarms of bees
Lodge two feet above your knees,
'Cause you rumbled holy women in the hay.

May a consumptive cobbler castrate you on a
red-hot last.

That Cromwell's corpse may rise again and
give you good looks.

Curse the man who twists his lips
When with you hot punch he sips;
Curse him twice if bread he breaks
Gosthering on like Kelly's drakes.
Curse him if you see him scratch
When you take him 'neath your thatch;
For the shifty, grey-faced swine
Will be gone at half-past-nine.
Curse him every day you waken
For your woman he'll have taken.

That you may be left a hundred pounds and the will lost.

May you starve till you can kiss a goat between the horns.

That you may spend your days burning tarred
rope in a bucket and squatting on it.
(*Regarded as a cure for piles.*)

May there be only a cripple around to get the
priest for you.

That your feet may have blisters when they're
dancing the angel's hornpipe.

May you croak, confound you, and may you
get the pip.
(*A disease in fowl.*)

The devil go with you and sixpence and then you'll never want for company or money.

Six eggs to you and a half-dozen of them rotten.

May you have nothing in your bag at the going down of the sun and less when it rises.

Don't starve the scald-crows – die in a ditch next winter.

May your last hornpipe be in the air.
(*May you hang.*)

Here's my gift for you:
A useless, useful instrument;
Bought for money, it cannot be lent.
Although you now own it, it isn't your own
But I hope that it soon will carry you home.
(*It is a coffin.*)

May you suffer everything that Cromwell might give except his money.

That the only full pockets you'll ever have be in your habit.

A curse on your house if you have one; if you haven't, blast the stars.

That you may melt off the earth like snow off a ditch and may there be a river of fire to catch you.

May the Lord call you when your master is away and his larder full.

Death and bad luck afterwards to you.

When the last train leaves for heaven may you still be in the waiting-room.

May your soul's transport be a lame jinnet with diarrhoea that's also fond of the fire.

When it rains gold, may you be without a spoon.

Coarse and Profane

St Patrick's curse on Ardagh to you: never without a liar, a rogue and a whore.

Shag you, you whore's melt.

The curse of Jesus Christ on a whore-house on you.

Blast you to hell, you poxy go-by-the-road.

May your obituary be written in weasel's piss.

That you may shit sideways.

May the devil swallow you sideways and choke on your pecker.

May the lamb of God stir his hoof through the roof of heaven and kick you in the arse down to hell.

(*John M. Feehan*)

May the devil cut your genitals out and feed them to the pigs.
(*Ibid.*)

Be the twenty-four balls of the twelve apostles.
(*Ibid.*)

May the devil put his hoof far up your arse and drag the ferrule of your hole below your knee!

The devil roast the balls off you and skewer them.

Be the scurvy spittle of a drunken hoor!

That the skin of your pecker may fester.

That you may ride the divil's wife and she with glass inside her.

May Old Nick's balls bounce on your bed,
His spittle stain your pillow.
And may you ever sleep in dread
Of his big, black, wobbly willow.

That you may marry a get who would be a bastard even if his parents married.

A landlord's pox on you and yours.

May you get a witch's syphilis from your broom handle!

That your arse may close up.
Answer: Yours cannot, for you're always talking through it.

Wherever you go, may you be as welcome as a fart in a telephone kiosk.

May your woman be frigid, your Ned knotted and may you be filled with bad thoughts.

When she gave it to you
She gave it to others;
May she give to you
What she gave to others.
When she gave it to others,
She has it.
If she has, may you get it.
If you get it, you get,
Then bejaysus – you've had it.
And so be it, you git!

Blast you for a tinker; may you be wandering
hungry till your ankles wear up to your balls;
and may your mangy dog eat what's left and
leave you with rabies as well.

A curse on Parnell and Tim Healy as well
On Members of Parliament, snooty and swell;
A curse on Dick Pigott, who told of the vice
Between Kitty O'Shea and the leader of lice.
May Avondale's blackbird, lose pecker and
    bone
Be they crushed 'neath the weight of decrepit
    Gladstone.

May the divil gulp you so far down his throat
that you'll have to shove your toothbrush up
his arse to clean your teeth.

With all your money, airs and graces, may you
be left where the crows don't shite.

May the hairs on your arse turn into drumsticks and beat the shite out of you.

Blast the slimy, two-faced get; he's so far up my arse I can taste him.

After my final visit to the Department of Folklore in University College Dublin, I had occasion to visit a student's lavatory. I noticed the following piece of graffiti there:

May your pubes go up in flames and your balls burn.

(The future of the coarse curse is in safe hands!)

Curses from Poets and Writers

Lord, confound this surly sister,
Blight her brow with blotch and blister,
Cramp her larynx, lung and liver,
In her guts a galling give her.
Let her live to earn her dinners
In Mountjoy with seedy sinners:
Lord, this judgement quickly bring,
And I'm Your servant, J. M. Synge.

(*J. M. Synge, 'The Curse'. To a sister of an enemy of Synge's who disapproved of his play,* The Playboy of the Western World.)

Death to every foe and traitor!

(*John Keegan Casey, 'The Rising of the Moon'*)

Oh I curse the stifling, smothering breath of
the religion that withered my loving and my
living and my womanhood.

(*John B. Keane*, Big Maggie, *Finale*)

Heart's blood and bowels' blood!
May your eyes go blind
And your knees be broken! ...
Destruction pursue you,
Morris the traitor,
Who brought death to my husband!

(*Eileen O'Leary, 'The Lament for Art Ó Laoghaire', trans.
Frank O'Connor.*)

God rot him and his children.

(*Ibid.*)

May nothing good come to them
But slaughter and terror
Until they are spent.
Nor halt or adjustment assist;
May no rock, hill or mountain offer shelter;
That their lives may be like the hunted fox or
    game.
(*From the Irish, Máire Bhuí Ní Láoire, 'Cath Cheím an
Fhía'*)

My grief on the sea, 'tis it that's huge
Swelling twixt me and my darling.
(*From the Irish. Anon., 'Mo Bhrón ar an bhFarraige'*)

BIBLIOGRAPHY

Journals and Manuscripts

Béaloideas: The Journal of the Folklore Society of Ireland, Vols 1–49

Irish Folklore Collection, the Department of Irish Folklore, University College, Dublin

Books

de h-Íde, Dubhglas, *Amhain Chúige Chonnacht: An Leath Rann* (Baile Átha Cliath 1922)

Colum, Padraic, *A Treasury of Irish Folklore* (New York 1967)

Dodds, E. R. (ed.), *The Collected Poems of Louis MacNeice* (London, 1979)

Feehan, John, *My Village, My World* (Cork and Dublin 1992)

Graves, A. P., *Songs of Killarney* (London 1873)

Hyde, Douglas, *The Religious Songs of Connaught,* Vol. 2 (Dublin and London 1922)